W9-BDH-555

CARING
It's Not a Spectator Sport

LILYA WAGNER

Pacific Press®
Publishing Association

Nampa, Idaho | Oshawa, Ontario, Canada
www.pacificpress.com

Cover design by Steve Lanto
Cover design resources from iStockphoto.com
Inside design by Kristin Hansen-Mellish

The authors assume full responsibility for the accuracy of all facts and quotations as cited in this book.

Unless otherwise noted, scriptures are quoted from *The Living Bible,* copyright © 1971 by Tyndale House Publishers, Wheaton, IL. Used by permission.

Scripture quotations marked KJV are from the King James Version.

Scriptures marked NASB are from *The New American Standard Bible*®, copyright © 1960, 1962, 1963, 1968, 1971, 1972, 1973, 1975, 1977, 1995 by The Lockman Foundation. Used by permission.

Scripture quotations marked NIV are from the HOLY BIBLE, NEW INTERNATIONAL VERSION®. Copyright © 1973, 1978, 1984 by International Bible Society. Used by permission of Zondervan Publishing House. All rights reserved.

You can obtain additional copies of this book by calling toll-free 1-800-765-6955 or by visiting http://www.adventistbookcenter.com.

Library of Congress Cataloging-in-Publication Data:

Wagner, Lilya.
  [Caring is not a spectator sport]
  Caring : it's not a spectator sport / by Lilya Wagner with Hal Thomsen.
    pages cm
  Rev. ed. of: Caring is not a spectator sport. c1986.
  ISBN 13: 978-0-8163-2892-5 (pbk.)
  ISBN 10: 0-8163-2892-7 (pbk.)
1. Caring—Religious aspects—Christianity. I. Title.
BV4647.S9W34 2014
241'.4—dc23
                                    2014018853

July 2014

Acknowledgments

Many thanks to Cheerie Lou Capman who ably edited the manuscript, and to the many compassionate and action-oriented people who provided the living examples in this book.

Contents

Chapter 1

The Problem of Compassion Fatigue

E ddie joined our student body during his senior year. Just what kind of home had produced such a misfit, we never did learn. Just what circumstances had shaped him, we never did find out. But Eddie quickly earned notoriety as the most obnoxious kid on campus. He was definitely the worst misfit we had that year.

Awkward, wearing clothes that didn't fit, always a silly grin on his face, Eddie never seemed to know what to say. So he said things that were far from sensible and always earned him ridicule, even if muffled and disguised.

Eddie graduated and dropped out of sight. No one cared— not even the alumni office soliciting funds for a new organ. Eddie wouldn't have been successful enough to contribute anything, we thought.

About ten years later, Eddie surfaced again. A former faculty member bumped into him unexpectedly. They exchanged the usual pleasantries. Nothing much had changed—Eddie still fidgeted, said the wrong things, and needed a shower. Rejection, hurt, and self-distrust reflected from his pale blue eyes.

Only a few nights after the chance meeting, the teacher's phone rang. "This is Eddie," the voice mumbled. "I've just taken enough of an overdose to kill me. I'm at a McDonald's—if anyone is interested."

Eddie survived that one, then faded into obscurity once again. Few of us thought much about him, even when it came to alumni lists.

In 1975, when the United States–backed government collapsed in Cambodia, black-clad Khmer Rouge swarmed down from their mountain hideouts and took over the cities and countryside. Cambodians greeted their arrival with enthusiasm, declaring, "A new era has begun! We're being liberated from war by our own countrymen!"

The enthusiasm quickly faded and turned to horror as the Khmer Rouge, under the leadership of a French-educated college professor called Pol Pot, began a reign of terror. Cities were emptied, and anyone who resisted was tortured, mutilated, and finally killed. Soldiers herded the population into the countryside and forced everyone to work there at gunpoint.

Civilization fell aside as a cordon of silence surrounded the country. Only in 1979, when the regime collapsed with the invasion of the Vietnamese, did the rest of the world learn of the holocaust that had taken place. Approximately a third of Cambodia's population perished, either from starvation or the mass killings.

Refugees poured into camps in Thailand; there they tried to pick up the shattered pieces of their lives. Few families remained intact. Many were ill; all were destitute. The survivors of this massacre had nightmares of times they wanted to forget, yet couldn't.

In the camps, they received meager food rations, sometimes learned a trade, and sometimes attended English and Bible classes. They were a people in limbo because they had been declared illegal immigrants; they didn't have many rights that refugees can claim.

Eventually, some were repatriated, some languished in camps month after month in a state of uncertainty, some were shuffled from camp to camp in a sometimes futile effort to control the refugee problem, and some made it to the United States or another welcoming country.

One of these refugees, Malypon, wrote to a former teacher:

> Dear teacher: How are you? I hope you are well. You are my good teacher and friend. I am missing you.
>
> On the twenty-seventh of last month we arrived at this camp at one o'clock in the morning. Here we have a small room, smaller than at the Ubon camp. There are twenty-five persons per lavatory. There are about 15,000 refugees and 171 buildings.
>
> The big problem of us is that there is not enough water, all day long. There are many long lines of people who wait for water from water tanks. Some day we get only three to four buckets. It is not enough for eating and washing.
>
> As you know, refugees in this camp can't go to third country. We live day by day. Have no dreams, smile, or song. I've been here for about two weeks, but it seems a long time.
>
> We are worry about our future; no man ever saw the future, we don't know what the future may bring forth—happy or sad?
>
> This is the first English letter of me, if I wrote wrong please correct me.

This example has been repeated numerous times in the ensuing years since the Cambodian holocaust—too many times for people like Malypon. They wait while most of the world turns its attention to yet another explosive spot that will breed even more refugees.

The screaming ambulance whisked José to the emergency room of the small hospital. As he lay among all that white sterility, panic and confusion mixed with the pain on his face. This was more than he had bargained for when he accepted the gilded offer to make money in the United States. Back in his country, he may not have been wealthy, but here he lived in a barren shack with twenty other people and worked himself to exhaustion for an income that usually ranked at half the government's official poverty income level. He suffered through each day with sweat pouring off him and no sanitary place to get a drink.

He couldn't communicate—he hadn't been in Florida long enough to learn how to speak adequate English. He couldn't understand or answer the questions fired at him: "What happened?" "Are you allergic to any medication?" "Who can we call?" Then someone came in who could translate from English to Spanish— and what relief flowed over José's face!

José and a friend had been hacking away at the dense undergrowth of an orange grove with their machetes, when his friend's tool had slipped. It nearly severed José's hand.

In time, of course, José's hand healed, and he slipped away, again joining the ranks of the thousands of underprivileged, overworked, underpaid laborers who trek across the United States in search of a way to make a living and support their families, or send money back to their countries of origin.

Some time ago, two men looking for a lost dog came across a cardboard shack in the woods near their homes. Thinking someone had simply piled trash in that part of the woods, they decided to have some fun target shooting. After a few shots, they stared in disbelief as an emaciated old man crept out of the box, scared by the bullets.

Sixty-one-year-old Johnson had lived with a sister but couldn't get along with the man she married, so he had moved into his own makeshift shack built from materials he'd found by the roadside. He said he scrounged food and clothing from dumpsters.

His case confounded the social workers in the nearest town. Where would they put him? Already the genuine but inadequate efforts of relief agencies couldn't meet the needs of other homeless like him. But certainly he couldn't go on living as he had, they all agreed.

The landscape is bleak. Figures that look like the stick people a child might draw dot the horizon. As they draw nearer, their faces and bodies take on a horrifying similarity. All are starving. Some mothers have lost almost all their children and cling to the one emaciated child that remains.

Drought has affected many countries, and the resulting famines cause many deaths, such as the 2011–2012 drought in East Africa. In turn, even the livestock suffer and die, causing mass migrations that produce refugees who stream into countries that aren't always able to sustain their own populations. Often the end result is violence by desperate people who clash with those who may have more but can't or aren't willing to share.

Images of starving children and adults have flashed across television screens and haunted the pages of news magazines. The United Nations Food and Agriculture Organization estimated that nearly 870 million people of the 7.1 billion people in the world, or one in eight, were suffering from chronic undernourishment in 2010–2012. Almost all the hungry people, 852 million, live in developing countries, representing 15 percent of the population of developing counties. There are 16 million people undernourished in developed countries.

Dee's first memories of life are of a strong light shining in her face as she lay in her crib and an angry voice shouting at her. "Forty years ago," she says, "people didn't know what to do about child abuse cases." So Dee is damaged for life, physically as well as psychologically.

Dee's parents deny having done anything to her. This haunts her.

"I know I didn't imagine it," she says, sadness creeping over her scarred face and tears filling her eyes. She tells of how her father would come in from working on the farm, become angry at something unknown to Dee, hurl her to the floor, then jump on her while still wearing his workboots.

When Red Cross workers suspected something was wrong with the child, they took Dee to doctors, who performed corrective surgery. "I didn't need the surgery, except that my parents had abused me so badly," Dee remembers. They often left Dee alone—a small, undersized child who had to walk with crutches. They also left something else, a newspaper through which tacks had been pushed. The newspaper lay on the floor, the sharp points of the tacks protruding upward. As expected, Dee stumbled and nearly gouged out an eye. For this, she was punished severely.

At forty-four years of age, Dee asks, "Why does society make me pay even more for something I didn't deserve?" Most of the time she is ignored, misunderstood, and labeled as mentally unstable. Somehow, she survives.

Call them disadvantaged, unfortunate, abused, displaced, or mistreated. Whether refugees, abused children, or street people—hungry, homeless, or hurting—they are with us. The faceless statistics are overwhelming.

These statistics include refugees. The latest figures available indicate that the estimated total number of refugees stood at 10.4 million at the beginning of 2013. Civil war, brutality, starvation, economic disaster—all contribute to this flow of people seeking asylum and assistance. As a poignant United Nations High Commissioner for Refugees billboard in an airport stated, "Going Home Tonight? Millions of refugees wish they could." Indeed, as a refugee myself, I can identify well with the desire for a home and with the loss of all possessions, family, country, livelihoods, and other aspects of life many take for granted.

Homelessness is the other side of the refugee picture, with an estimated annual number of homeless between 2.3 and 3.5 million, including children. The causes are many, including loss of jobs and income, abuse, mental illness, post-traumatic stress disorder, and substance abuse. Children in the United States are suffering from a hidden epidemic of child abuse and neglect. On the average, every year more than three million reports of child abuse are made in the United States involving more than six million children (a report can include multiple children). The United States has one of the worst records among industrialized nations—losing on average between four and seven children every day to child abuse and neglect. Children who suffer many kinds of abuse end up in foster homes, institutions, or on the streets, and perpetuate the cycle that forced them to endure this kind of life. They become statistics that swell into faceless misery.

These are the dramatic cases, the hurts that attract public attention. Many others suffer from such problems as alcoholism, spouse abuse, loneliness, or illness. Many situations that bring hurt and many people who need help do not capture public attention.

Bertrand Russell, the English philosopher known for his studies in logic and mathematics as well as his essays and lectures on philosophy, wrote in his autobiography: "Three passions, simple but overwhelmingly strong, have governed my life." The first two were a longing for love and a search for knowledge. The third, he said, was "unbearable pity for the suffering of mankind." He added, "Echoes of cries of pain reverberate in my heart."

These same echoes also reach our ears in such a stream and with such intensity that perhaps we have lost our capacity to hear them. We who are not crying in pain perhaps have become desensitized to the sensory and emotional stimuli. Perhaps we have become selectively deaf to certain frequencies because the receptors in our hearts have been destroyed or no longer function.

Christian ears and hearts should not be desensitized, and yet sometimes it seems this is a prevalent condition, if only because we don't know what to do about those "echoes of cries of pain."

The faceless statistics are overwhelming and disturbing. We may feel compelled to do something but may instead succumb to compassion fatigue. Yet we can't afford to sit on the sidelines, oblivious to the suffering, deprivation, and desperation around us. We can't afford to be apathetic, just because those faceless statistics are far away and impersonal. We can't afford to remain insensitive, because we have moral, humanitarian, and Christian obligations to fulfill.

But, most important, we can't afford to remain uninvolved, because Jesus showed us that caring is not a spectator sport!

Chapter 2

Jesus and the Power of Compassion

J esse Carpenter, a sixty-one-year-old derelict, froze to death on a cold December night in a park that faced the White House, yet he was buried in Arlington National Cemetery with military honors and a twenty-one-gun salute. Carpenter would have died the typically anonymous death of a street person, except that his ex-wife saw a newspaper account of his death and sent his Bronze Star certificate to Washington.

Carpenter fought in World War II in France and was awarded the Bronze Star for carrying wounded comrades to safety while under German gun fire. He returned home as a wartime hero, but this honor couldn't help him adjust to normal life, and he became an alcoholic. For twenty-two years, he wandered through city streets, homeless but not friendless.

Those who knew Carpenter thought he was as much a hero then as during World War II, yet he received no medals for his deeds. He was known as a gentle man, one who did all he could to help others even less fortunate than he. For two years before his death, Carpenter spent most of his time pushing a wheelchair. He died at the feet of his buddy, John Lam, who was helpless because of Parkinson's disease. Ignored and invisible while alive, Carpenter was eulogized at his funeral for his compassion, gentleness, and thoughtfulness. He became a symbol for the struggle in providing better care for the city's homeless.

Carpenter, a wino, was a nobody, yet he had a capacity to see pain and suffering and do something about it. In this he, perhaps unknowingly, reflected the best example we have of a caring and compassionate life—the life of Jesus.

Matthew must have been deeply impressed and moved by the compassion he saw in Jesus, because he recorded a series of occasions when Jesus cared and put that caring into action. In that portion of his writings we now call chapter 9, he first tells about Jesus' healing of the paralytic. We need to notice that Jesus didn't just glibly say, "Pick up your stretcher, and go on home, for you are healed," but He saw the inner torment of a man who wanted forgiveness for a sordid life even more than he wanted physical healing.

Just after this miraculous event, Matthew records something very personal. He tells how Jesus saw him sitting by the road, doing a job the Jews despised—collecting taxes. This line of work definitely made Matthew a shunned and despised citizen. Matthew reports that Jesus said, "Come and be my disciple," and he records his own reaction: "Matthew jumped up and went along with him."

But Christ's involvement didn't stop there; He and His disciples had dinner at Matthew's house. Matthew himself says that many notorious swindlers were guests at the dinner. Of course, this drew the attention of Jesus' most active critics, and they asked His disciples, "Why does your teacher associate with men like that?"

Then Jesus wasted no words in telling them plainly that people who are well don't need a doctor, but sick people do. And He added, "It isn't your sacrifices and your gifts I want—I want you to be merciful."

Matthew then reports how Jesus resurrected the daughter of a rabbi from the local synagogue. On the way to the man's house,

Matthew noted, a woman who simply touched Jesus' clothing was healed—a woman who had been sick for twelve years. Then when Jesus left the rabbi's home, after actually raising the little girl from death, He healed two blind men. Finally, Matthew tells about how Jesus cast out a demon from a mute man. He says that the crowds marveled. "Never in all our lives have we seen anything like this," they exclaimed.

Matthew ends this series of reports by saying that Jesus traveled through the area announcing the good news about the kingdom, adding that wherever He went He healed people of every sort of illness. Finally, Matthew writes those key words, "But when he saw the multitudes, he was moved with compassion on them" (Matthew 9:36, KJV). Matthew must have been especially impressed by this, because he wrote this phrase at other times as well (Matthew 14:14).

Two points in this text should not escape our notice. First, Jesus *saw* the multitudes. It's so easy to become engrossed in our daily affairs and personal lives that we see little else. Jesus was no doubt as busy as we are; after all, think of His mission. He had an entire world to save. He could have easily become totally involved in preaching the good news of the kingdom.

But Jesus saw two equal sides to His ministry: ministering to the souls of people and ministering to their suffering. He saw these as equal sides of one task, because He had genuine compassion—holistic compassion—for humankind. When He defined His mission very early in His public life, He quoted from Isaiah: "The Spirit of the Lord is upon me, because . . . he hath sent me to heal the brokenhearted, to preach deliverance to the captives, and recovering of sight to the blind, to set at liberty them that are bruised" (Luke 4:18, KJV).

A second point to notice are the words "moved with compassion." The Greek word used for this phrase is the strongest word available for pity. It means compassion that literally comes from the bowels, meaning the inner depths of a person. In fact, this word is used only when speaking of Jesus or when quoting His parables. It literally means the deepest sense of caring that is possible for a human being to experience.

Jesus tackled His twofold mission with vigor. He saw people as God's created human beings who suffered from a long list of earthly maladies. These people weren't faceless statistics, to be ignored at will. He took the time and effort to know them as people.

Remember the story of the woman at the well? She was amazed that Jesus would speak to her, even in requesting something for Himself, because usually a Jew wouldn't stoop to ask a "despised Samaritan" for *anything*! Jesus didn't think about ingrained biases and cultural borders. He began telling her about the Water of Life.

Even His disciples were surprised that He would speak to a shunned woman. With His discerning wisdom, He knew she had led a sinful life. Certainly being married five times and currently living in sin wasn't much of a glowing background. But Jesus had such interest in helping her that He even forgot how hungry and thirsty He was. He took the time, He had the patience, to see beneath the surface of this disadvantaged woman.

In Jesus' day, lepers not only suffered the ravaging results of their disease, they also suffered from the loneliness of isolation. One authority has recorded that a leper could come no closer than fifty feet to a healthy person. Lepers also suffered psychologically, because the prevalent societal attitude held that leprosy struck as punishment for a sinful life.

Unlike His contemporaries, Jesus didn't panic and run when He heard the shouts of the ten lepers. He stopped, waited until they came closer, and even talked to them! Jesus then healed these ten men; but what happened? Only one came back to thank Him. Jesus knew as well as we do that all too often when people get what they want, they never come back—even with thanks. But that didn't keep Jesus from having compassion and putting that compassion into action.

On one occasion, Jesus and His disciples walked fifty miles to Tyre and Sidon. After they got there, they sat down to eat a welcome meal, but this was rudely interrupted. A Phoenician woman showed up, pleading that Jesus heal her daughter, who had an evil spirit. The disciples were apparently offended. After all, she was a woman and a foreigner! They wanted to get rid of her, and at first it looked as if Jesus was equally annoyed. He seemed to ignore her. However, she persisted, willingly admitting that though she might be a second-class citizen, even dogs usually received the crumbs from the master's table!

Jesus then paid special attention to her, expressing His admiration. "Your faith is large, and your request is granted," He said (Matthew 15:28). His disciples thought that, as a foreigner, she didn't merit His favors, but this didn't matter to Jesus. His seemingly uncaring attitude was only temporarily assumed, designed to teach His disciples an unforgettable lesson. After He had made His point, He saw, had compassion, and took action.

Zacchaeus was an outcast among his countrymen and despised by his neighbors. He not only worked as a tax collector, a job the Jews thought worse than cleaning a pig pen, but he was quite possibly an *unscrupulous* tax collector as well. Adding to these disadvantages, he was short and perhaps not very good looking. He had to climb a tree to see what was going on, and no doubt the leafy branches hid him quite well. Yet Jesus, through all the commotion of an admiring crowd, saw him—maybe even looked for him. Jesus stopped and astonished everyone when He invited Himself to lunch at Zacchaeus's house! He dared risk public scorn when He saw beneath the surface of an unattractive and hated person who engaged in a despised profession.

One day a woman accused of adultery was dragged to Jesus.

There was no doubt of her guilt—she'd been caught in the act. Normally, she would have been stoned on the spot, but because the Jewish leaders wanted to test and embarrass Jesus, they decided to prolong her inevitable fate. Jesus was not embarrassed by the sordid details. He even had the insight into humanity to discern that she was not the only guilty party present. He didn't condemn her; He simply counseled her to change her ways. Scholars believe this woman was Mary, the sister of Martha and Lazarus. If so, Jesus' compassionate action had far-reaching results, as she became one of His most loyal and active followers.

The Gospels are full of examples showing how Jesus *saw* and *had compassion.* When we study these passages, we see Jesus' compassion in action. His actions were on behalf of anyone who needed help—no one ever got lost in the crowd.

We can see Jesus' compassionate actions demonstrated in such ways as the following:

1. Jesus always longed to ease suffering—to heal. He had compassion for the sick, for the handicapped, and for those in the grip of demons.
2. Jesus wanted to alleviate hunger. When crowds that followed Him became tired and hungry, He used power He normally didn't call on. He couldn't be content with having enough for Himself when others suffered from hunger.
3. Jesus cared about the lonely. Whether loneliness was brought about by disease, as in the case of lepers or blind people, or whether loneliness was caused by societal stigmas, Jesus cared and went into action. Surely loneliness was as painful in His time as it is in ours.
4. Jesus cared about people's minds. He saw that many were concerned because the teachings of the Jewish leaders offered them little hope, much less enlightenment. He

countered this problem by avoiding theoretical discussions and preaching clear, example-filled sermonettes. He didn't avoid questions, particularly when asked by honest, searching individuals.

5. Jesus was moved by tears, and He didn't feel it beneath Him to weep with others. He cared when people mourned the death of loved ones. He cared when people were hurting because of physical and psychological trauma, and He took action whenever possible.

6. Jesus cared for individuals who suffered from any kind of earthly malady, whether they were foreigners, outcasts, poverty-stricken, unscrupulous professionals, or respected and wealthy individuals. Guidelines carefully set up by tradition and cultural expectations didn't matter. If He saw anyone hurting for any reason, He had compassion.

Jesus was hardly insensitive to the multitudes of His time—multitudes that included all segments of His society. He took His twofold mission very seriously. He ministered to people's souls, and He ministered to their suffering. He certainly must have been familiar with the many Old Testament injunctions such as this one, "Thus has the LORD of hosts said, 'Dispense true justice, and practice kindness and compassion each to his brother'" (Zechariah 7:9, NASB).

Jesus made clear what our Christian responsibility is, not only by His example but by a futuristic story He told about sheep and goats (Matthew 25). He pictures Himself on a throne, surrounded by masses of people divided into two groups.

In His analogy, He clarified a significant point. Just as a shepherd separates his sheep from the goats, so He, in His role as King, divides those people who had compassion from those who didn't. He then says to those whom He has gathered by His right hand, "Come, you who are blessed of My Father, inherit the kingdom prepared for you from the foundation of the world" (verse 34, NASB). Why were they invited into this choice position? Because, Jesus says, when He was hungry, they fed Him. When He was thirsty, they gave Him water. When He was a stranger, they eased His loneliness. When He was sick and in prison, they visited Him.

The symbolic sheep, at the honored position on His right, are astonished. They don't remember having performed such deeds. Then Jesus makes this emphatic statement: "When you did it to these my brothers, you were doing it to me!"

What about the symbolic goats? Jesus doesn't mince any words. "Away with you, you cursed ones!" This side is also astonished. They can't remember their lack of compassionate action, so Jesus says, "When you refused to help the least of these my brothers, you were refusing help to me."

We have Jesus as our personal Example. He never succumbed to compassion fatigue. He never even considered not caring. Peter, who must have observed Christ's marvelous displays of compassion firsthand, wrote some years later, "Finally, be ye all of one mind, having compassion one of another, love as brethren" (1 Peter 3:8, KJV). And John, the beloved disciple, wrote, "Let us stop just *saying* we love people; let us *really* love them, and *show it* by our *actions*" (1 John 3:18; emphasis in original).

It's easy to mingle with masses of people in places such as airports and shopping malls, while ignoring individuals. It's also easy to watch news happening in problem areas anywhere in the world, exclaim in pity, and forget the scene as soon as the television is turned off.

Only when we really begin to *see* as Jesus did can we begin to have *compassion* as He did. Only when we leave our place on the sidelines and stop being mere spectators can we have compassion as Jesus did.

Chapter 3

Blessed Are the Merciful

The lush green jungle almost hides the tiny, worn path that threads its way up the mountain and finally disappears in the tangled undergrowth. A man appears from this blend of greenery. Slowly, he walks closer, head bent. Finally, he sinks down by the side of the path, curls up in a fetal position, and draws his tattered shirt around himself.

Had we stood by this path, we would have observed this scene repeating itself too many times for our peace of mind. The man is starving, and because he has no resistance to disease, hunger and fever drop him on the trail.

Half a continent away, a gaunt, dark man kneels in the desert. His bony fingers dig into the dry sand. The sun lengthens his shadow as he bends over his task, and finally he is rewarded. A tiny trickle of water runs over his fingers. He smiles wearily and fills his jar. Behind him a dusty wind swirls around the meager huts and crowds of emaciated people. Children with distended bellies play, but their motions seem like those in a time-lapse film because they have no energy.

Scenes such as these speak of realities around the globe. One-third of the world's hungry live in India. Famine-stricken areas increasingly disgorge scores of people who flock to the cities, only to camp in railroad stations or on sidewalks, and finally die from disease and hunger.

In Bogota, Colombia, twelve thousand to thirteen thousand people are homeless, and 40 percent of these are children who prowl the streets and live in packs. They camp on the doorsteps of prosperous businesses and huddle in alleys by small fires. Begging, stealing, working for the lowest wages possible, they survive.

The early years of the twenty-first century saw massive disasters such as the tsunami in Southeast Asia, the Japanese and Haitian earthquakes, and the tsunami in the Philippines. These all have similar themes of enormous suffering—death, loss of loved ones, hunger, disease, destruction of a city's infrastructure and services, and the accompanying emotional upheaval.

Closer to home, we observe hunger, unemployment, and lack of housing, conditions exacerbated by disasters such as Hurricane Katrina and Hurricane Sandy. For many, these conditions linger and have become a way of life. A term has been coined by America's sociologists for a burgeoning segment of society that seems mired in poverty—a segment that is destitute, has few if any job skills, is plagued by alcohol and drug abuse, is elderly, or has a history of mental illness. This segment is called America's underclass.

Harsh winter winds call attention to a growing problem. More than half a million Americans live in rags and scavenge for food. These destitutes are found in most cities of any size.

For those who manage to survive by huddling over steam grates, finding temporary shelter in bus terminals or garages, or begging for handouts, life goes on. But the quality of that life is dehumanizing and atrocious.

Even closer to home lives a little girl of about eight. Her home is one of the shabbier places in a suburban area, but to the unknowing passerby she appears normal, if somewhat underprivileged. However, a discerning person would note that she is excessively nervous, wants yet shuns attention, and when she finally finds a stranger she feels she can trust, she thrusts her grubby little hand into the larger one and sighs, "I wish you were my mother."

Then her own mother leans through the screenless window and strongly commands, "Come inside! Don't bother people!" Someone who could read the signals of child abuse would recognize this little girl as a victim. Unfortunately, most don't recognize child abuse unless they are closely involved, and others don't know how to intervene.

Against this background, let's consider what Jesus really meant when He spoke the beatitude, "Blessed are the merciful" (Matthew 5:7, KJV). What does it mean to have mercy? Just what should a Christian do?

The Christian life is one that reflects the life and teachings of Jesus. Because He so willingly shared His mercy and kindness with us, we have the responsibility of recognizing this vast gift, of being sensitive to others' need for that mercy, and of sharing that mercy in turn.

Mercy is a frequently used word in the Old Testament. More than 150 references include it—most in connection with God and His actions. The word is most often used when speaking of God's relationship to mankind.

Mercy is demonstrated throughout history, as seen in the Exodus from Egypt described in Exodus 15:13 and Psalm 78. The psalmists often referred and appealed to God's mercy, as in Psalms 6 and 86, whether for deliverance from earthly dangers or for forgiveness of sins.

Evidence that God's mercy is abundant and lasts forever can be found in 1 Chronicles 16:34 and Psalm 136. Psalm 31 describes how mercy gives man joy in spite of trouble, and Psalm 94 talks about it as the source of human strength.

Mercy is readily displayed in many of the Bible stories of the

Old Testament, such as Lot's escape from Sodom, Jacob's dream of the heavenly ladder, Joseph's ordeal as a slave in Egypt, and David's deliverance from Saul. The frequent mention of God's mercy is just one indication of God's love for His people and His caring for their needs.

But the Old Testament is equally replete with the idea that because mercy is a characteristic of God's relationship to mankind, He also expects them to show mercy to fellow human beings. "Let not mercy and truth forsake thee," stated a wise man in Proverbs 3:3 (KJV), and Micah wrote that man's entire duty was to do justice, love mercy, and walk humbly before God (Micah 6:8).

The New Testament language does not speak of mercy as often, but its meaning is no less significant than in the Old Testament. Paul wrote in Ephesians 2:4 and Titus 3:5 that God is abundant in mercy and that mercy saves us. Jesus Himself elaborated on the concept of mercy when He told the story of the good Samaritan (see the next chapter). He wanted mercy to be an outreach of love.

Jesus' mercy toward people, which showed itself in action while here on earth, is better evaluated when seen in the context of His era. In Roman times, unwanted children, especially females, were simply allowed to die of exposure. People from conquered nations were enslaved and treated worse than property and livestock. A slave could be flogged or killed for something as insignificant as dropping a prized vase. Rebellious slaves and other insurgents were crucified by the score. Man's inhumanity towards mankind seemed at its height during Roman rule.

Jews displayed an appalling lack of mercy themselves while under subjugation to Rome. Jewish laws actually prescribed a lack of mercy to Gentiles, even in withholding medical help and nourishment.

As Jesus worked in this setting, His actions of mercy must

have astonished and confounded many. His stories were full of examples of mercy and underscored man's obligation to follow these examples. He told the story of the unmerciful servant who would not forgive a lesser debt even though the king had released him from the obligation of a much greater sum. In commenting on the wretched servant, Jesus had the king saying, "I forgave you all that tremendous debt, just because you asked me to—shouldn't you have mercy on others, just as I had mercy on you?" (Matthew 18:32, 33).

Jesus' entire life was an example of compassionate action, from the time He saved a wedding party from a disastrous ending, until His own testing in the Garden of Gethsemane when He prayed, "Not my will, but thine, be done" (Luke 22:42, KJV). He cared so much about us that He laid down His life on our behalf.

But Jesus also said, "For unto whomsoever much is given, of him shall be much required" (Luke 12:48, KJV). God expects, figuratively speaking, to get His money's worth out of His sacrifice and His display of mercy toward us. Divine love always makes its most touching appeals when it calls on us to show to others the same love and compassion that Christ displayed.

Mercy is not just having a feeling for others or making a sentimental statement of compassion. A cartoon drawn by Charles Schulz, creator of Peanuts, perhaps illustrates this best. Snoopy sits alone during a snowstorm, shivering. Charlie Brown and Linus, dressed in bulky and obviously warm coats, come over. They pat him on the head while Charlie says, "Be of good cheer," and Linus echoes, "Yes, be of good cheer." They leave, and Snoopy shivers on, a puzzled look on his face.

Mercy must be displayed in action, and that action is the opposite of self-centeredness and selfishness. Love of self is replaced by love for God, and this love therefore spills out to other people. True mercy is the essence of true religion.

Real religion is a way of life, not a mantle that we wrap around ourselves on Sabbath and then hang in a closet the rest of the week. True worship means working together with Christ and is shown by good works—by caring for the needy, fatherless, and widows.

Sometimes Christians display appalling insensitivity to the plight of others, even to the point of misquoting the injunction God gave the Israelites. "Didn't the Lord say, 'The poor always ye have with you'? So there's really nothing we can do," is a disturbing comment heard all too often (John 12:8, KJV). What these insensitive Christians forget is the rest of the verse, which says, "Therefore I command thee, saying, Thou shalt open thine hand wide unto thy brother, to thy poor, and to thy needy, in thy land" (Deuteronomy 15:11, KJV).

Ellen G. White expressed concern over compassion fatigue long ago when she wrote the following: "From what has been shown me, Sabbathkeepers are growing more selfish as they increase in riches. Their love for Christ and His people is decreasing. They do not see the wants of the needy, nor feel their sufferings or sorrows. They do not realize that in neglecting the poor and the suffering they neglect Christ, and that in relieving the wants and sufferings of the poor as far as possible, they minister to Jesus."[1]

The problem isn't that some people seem more blessed with money, health, enjoyment, and companionship than others. The problem is that a state of well-being, whether economic or physical, can often make us forget God. This causes a chain reaction, because then we forget God's mercy toward us and also fail to share this mercy.

To claim to be a true Christian while lacking compassion is hypocrisy. True religion is not simply an expression of piety or a form of religious practice. God spoke through Amos in condemning the callous attitude of that time and said, "I hate your show and your pretense—your hypocrisy" (Amos 5:21).

The relationship between religious faith and compassionate action cannot be broken. Here, again, Jesus was our best Example, and Luke, who chronicled His compassionate life, quotes Jesus as saying, "Try to show as much compassion as your Father does" (Luke 6:36).

James used some forceful yet beautiful language when he discussed the close relationship of faith and works: "Dear brothers, what's the use of saying that you have faith and are Christians if you aren't proving it by helping others? . . . Faith that doesn't show itself by good works is no faith at all—it is dead and useless" (James 2:14–17).

So our "good works" should include the mercy and compassionate action that Jesus displayed. This means developing the ability to feel what the other person feels, to empathize as well as to sympathize. Often we become so concerned with our own activities, our inner selves, our thoughts and feelings, that we feel no more than a twinge of compassion accompanied perhaps by a twinge of guilt.

It should be easy for us as Christians to develop empathy for those who are loosely labeled as "less fortunate." Like the poverty-stricken, we may be poor in spirit—poor in receiving the wants we so much yearn for, poor in a fulfilled, happy life. Like the foreigners, aliens, and refugees, we are not at home on this planet but are exiled from our heavenly home. Like the handicapped, we often lack skills or opportunities that we desire. Like the widows and orphans, we also have been hurt by human relationships or the loss of beloved friends and family. Like the oppressed, we have, at one time or another, not been free to do or speak as we wish, even if in a minor way.

When we keep in mind that we actually can think and feel like the disadvantaged, then we can have empathy. We can have identification, understanding, pity—and, at the same time, be moved to action.

George is a mentally retarded young man who lives in a rather ramshackle home for those who have "fallen through the cracks of society," as a friend puts it. George once had a mother and sister; little is known of his father. While growing up, George tried very hard to fit into the elementary school crowd, but he never got past first grade. George's mother, frustrated by having to care for someone who couldn't learn and obey like other children, tended to let him wander through the neighborhood. When George grew older, he had to leave home because his mother's new husband couldn't tolerate him. Undoubtedly, George was hard to love.

George will easily cling to the first person who speaks to him or shows any caring attitude. His blue eyes are intense, he hunches over as if in fear of a blow, and his hands move nervously. It's hard to like George, because he lacks social skills, evidently bathes infrequently, and seldom carries a tissue for his perpetually runny nose. Besides, he needs love and attention so much that he becomes a pest.

To help George, we must learn to have empathy. In many ways, aren't we like George? We hardly measure up to God's expectations for us and to the possibilities within us, when it comes to both mental and spiritual development. We've been scarred by some of life's hurts. And how many of us really know the right thing to say or do at the right time?

The mercy beatitude Jesus spoke that day when He shared so many Christian concepts ends with a promise—"they shall obtain mercy." If we fulfill our obligation to be merciful and compassionate, we place ourselves where we can receive God's mercy most abundantly. If we fail to practice compassion and mercy, we distance ourselves from God—and thus from His mercy as well.

As Isaiah put it, "Feed the hungry! Help those in trouble! Then your light will shine out from the darkness, and the darkness around you shall be as bright as day. And the Lord will guide you continually, and satisfy you with all good things, and keep you healthy too" (Isaiah 58:10, 11).

This beatitude, "Blessed are the merciful: for they shall obtain mercy," is a promise, a blessing, an injunction, and a warning all at the same time. And above all, it is a challenge to the compassionate, caring, involved Christian!

Endnote

1. Ellen G. White, *Testimonies for the Church* (Mountain View, Calif.: Pacific Press® Pub. Assn., 1948), vol. 2, 24.

Chapter 4

The Stranger Who
Taught Compassion

One day an expert on Moses' laws came to test Jesus and asked Him, "Teacher, what does a man need to do to live forever in heaven?" Jesus turned and answered him with a question, "What does Moses' law say about it?"

"It says," the interrogator stated without hesitation, "that you must love the Lord your God with all your heart, and with all your soul, and with all your strength, and with all your mind. And you must love your neighbor just as much as you love yourself." He had no trouble with the answer. After all, he was an expert in the law of Moses!

Then Jesus replied, "Right! Do this and you will live forever in heaven."

The man didn't care for this broad of an answer. Like most of his fellow Jews, he wanted to justify his lack of love for certain kinds of people, so he pretended ignorance and asked, "Who is my neighbor?" Jesus knew, and often used, one of the most effective means for getting across a point: He told a story.

"A man was going down from Jerusalem to Jericho,

when he was attacked by robbers. They stripped him of his clothes, beat him and went away, leaving him half dead. A priest happened to be going down the same road, and when he saw the man, he passed by on the other side. So too, a Levite, when he came to the place and saw him, passed by on the other side. But a Samaritan, as he traveled, came where the man was; and when he saw him, he took pity on him. He went to him and bandaged his wounds, pouring on oil and wine. Then he put the man on his own donkey, brought him to an inn and took care of him. The next day he took out two denarii and gave them to the innkeeper. 'Look after him,' he said, 'and when I return, I will reimburse you for any extra expense you may have.'

"Which of these three do you think was a neighbor to the man who fell into the hands of robbers?"

The expert in the law replied, "The one who had mercy on him."

Jesus told him, "Go and do likewise" (Luke 10:30–37, NIV).

Like any good piece of literature, Jesus' story had many details that only made the basic point more vivid. He chose a dramatic setting. Jesus' listeners knew that the road from Jerusalem to Jericho was treacherous. Jerusalem lies at 2,600 feet above sea level, and Jericho is 820 feet below sea level, so in less than 20 miles, the road drops more than 3,400 feet. This steep path was narrow and rocky, with sudden turns that made it an ideal place for robberies and murders.

People usually traveled this route in groups, but the traveler in Jesus' story was foolhardy and reckless. He chose to go alone. True, so did the other characters, but this man gambled and lost.

Jesus also chose interesting characters, easily identified by His audience. The priest, highly honored in the religious world of the Jews, came across the unfortunate traveler, looked at him, crossed to the other side of the road, and hurried on. Maybe his actions were guided by the fact that if he touched a dead man (and the man certainly looked dead) he would lose his turn for temple duty. No doubt this meant a great deal to him—all that pomp and glory—so he hastened on.

The temple assistant, or Levite, seemed to take more of an interest. Perhaps he did so because traditionally the role of Levites was to care for human needs. He approached the body, then hesitated. Maybe he remembered that bandits sometimes used decoys, even as today roadside motorists in distress are not always what they appear to be. He feared that if he stooped to help the man, he would be in a vulnerable position. So he didn't take the risk, and he hurried on.

Then the Samaritan came on the scene. Jesus' listeners probably thought the villain had arrived. A Samaritan was not only one who belonged to that race, but it was a derogatory term used for anyone who was different and despised. Imagine the audience's surprise when they discover that the Samaritan is the only one who cares about the wounded and dying Jew!

Why did this man care enough to respond to the needs of a stranger, at great risk to himself? What made him different from the others who ignored human need in the form of the beaten and robbed figure lying by the side of the road? By analyzing this unknown Samaritan, maybe we can uncover a fairly accurate portrait of him.

He must have been quite fearless or, better yet, courageous. Right before him, on this notably treacherous road, was evidence of the cruel and vicious acts that often took place. But he stopped to help. He was also courageous because he was willing to help an enemy—an enemy who would shun him and insult him in public if conditions and circumstances were different.

The antipathy between Jews and Samaritans dated back for centuries before this story took place. Samaritans, the Jews thought, did not have as pure of a religion as the Jews. Samaritans were thought to be insincere because they identified with the Jews when times were good but denied any connection with them when times were bad. The Jews, on the other hand, had shunned the Samaritans repeatedly for at least seven hundred years and condemned them for imagined or real infractions of pure religion (although many basic tenets of both religions were similar). But the good Samaritan demonstrated that people will be judged not by what they believe but by what they live. He had the courage to stop and make himself vulnerable to both assault and insult.

He had made caring a habit, probably one that he displayed openly and unashamedly. There is nothing weak about a caring person—especially if such behavior has become a habit. One doesn't just happen on occasions that call for caring and react with action any more than one hears the chirp of a cricket above the noise of traffic unless one is attuned to it. A habit of any kind must be developed. Conscious effort, frequent practice, repeated action and, at last, an action becomes virtually automatic.

This Samaritan must have been the kind who would rescue a cat stuck in a tree, fill a frail and elderly woman's pitcher with water, or comfort a child who had been bucked off a donkey. He probably remembered his mother on her birthday!

He was practical. He didn't waste time pondering or analyzing the situation but attended to the man's wounds right away. He apparently knew what kind of first aid to give, since the unfortunate traveler didn't die from the severe beating. Remember, he was in bad enough condition that the other passersby thought he was dead. Neither did the Samaritan wait for someone else to come by who might have an extra donkey or horse. He put the victim on his own means of transportation and walked, resulting in a much slower pace. He also realized the victim needed rest and care—and he made sure the man received it.

He was unselfish. No hint exists that he enjoyed social status or riches, but he nonetheless paid for the victim's room, board, and care. Comparatively speaking, he probably spent as much as we would today were we to pay for a good motel room and nursing care for someone in distress.

He was a man of action. He didn't just stand by and say, "Poor guy. Too bad." He got busy right away, doing what was needed. Besides, he nursed the wounded man through the first critical night, the story says.

He had empathy—that keen ability to not only express sorrow and show concern but actually to feel what the other person feels. When he saw the man lying by the side of the road, he could feel what it must be like to experience this kind of calamity.

He forgot his ethnic background, ignored the labels often attached to him (heretic, villain, outcast), and forgot age-old animosities. He simply saw the dying traveler as a fellow human being and had the inner strength to act as Jesus would have. Did he personally know Jesus? Possibly, yet probably not. What motivated him could have been a deep inner sense of responsibility to show compassion.

He was, perhaps, good looking—though not necessarily grand in outward appearance. What a person is inside reflects on the outside. As the wise writer of Proverbs 19:22 said, "Kindness makes a man attractive." Whether or not he had wavy black hair and a strong, straight nose, we don't know. Whether or not he was tall and just suntanned and muscular enough to be attractive, we also don't know. We can be reasonably sure, however, that his appearance was both arresting and intriguing—an appearance that probably didn't escape notice.

The good Samaritan cared. He obviously knew how to share that gift of caring—a gift that benefited not only others but himself as well. He must have fostered the same philosophy as that of Stephen Grellet, a New Jersey Quaker who died in 1855. This obscure Friend wrote, "I expect to pass through this world but once; any good thing therefore that I can do, or any kindness that I can show to any fellow creature, let me do it now; let me not defer or neglect it, for I shall not pass this way again."

Jesus had an underlying theme and purpose in telling this story. The Jews had narrowed their definition of *neighbor* to include only fellow Jews, so Jesus wanted to make a point about just who a neighbor might be. A neighbor is anyone who needs our help, even if he has caused his own problems, even if he is of a different nationality.

In telling the story of the good Samaritan, Jesus shared the truth that caring goes beyond simple pangs of pity. The good Samaritan got involved. He wasn't suffering from compassion fatigue. He cared, and he put that caring into action. When Jesus finished the story, He asked the question, "Now which of these three would you say was a neighbor to the bandits' victim?"

The questioner answered, "The one who showed him some pity."

No doubt Jesus then looked him squarely in the eye and let the significance of his own answer sink in. Finally, He said, "Yes, now go and do the same." Luke does not tell us what the man did, but that's not important. What is important is that we listen to Jesus' gentle command and apply it to ourselves.

Chapter 5

Compassion and the Power of Cooperation

The woman stood on the rooftop of her home and gazed toward the Mediterranean Sea. The white, pink, and blue houses surrounding hers were bathed in a flood of sunshine. Little silver-tipped waves reached out from the sea and caressed the small boats tied to the pier. Dorcas sighed; the view was certainly breathtaking.

Joppa, Dorcas's hometown, was Jerusalem's port, located approximately thirty miles northwest of Jerusalem itself. A very old city, Joppa was mentioned in historical writings as early as 1500 B.C. The name meant "beauty," and Joppa certainly deserved this designation. One look at the quaint city and the surrounding countryside was convincing enough.

The name of one of Joppa's prominent citizens also meant "beauty." Her Greek name, *Dorcas,* and her Aramaic name, *Tabitha,* were both translated as "gazelle." Because of the grace and beauty of this creature, the name was popular for a charming, attractive woman.

Dorcas, however, never lingered very long on her rooftop, savoring the view. Luke writes that she was "a believer who was always doing kind things for others, especially for the poor" (Acts 9:36). Dorcas was the center of her community and a central figure in the Christian church at Joppa. She must have led a busy life. Not merely a philanthropic worker, she was a true believer in caring for the needy of her city and time.

Because many ships sailed from this port city, there were also many calamities at sea. Joppa reportedly had more than a normal share of widows. Many of these women headed destitute families because their husbands had been lost at sea.

Dorcas was alert to the needs around her. She had pity and compassion as she observed the widows and orphans, and she became a one-woman welfare society. She worked hard and was known for her work, not for her wealth or social prominence. She combined her Christianity with social action, and, in this, she serves as a fine example in several ways.

First, Dorcas was "full of good works" (verse 36, KJV), meaning that she worked incessantly and untiringly. Second, her work was aimed at being useful. She succeeded because she was active and practical. She didn't engage in utopian or theoretical discussions; she simply went to work. Third, she worked humbly and for the humble. She did the Lord's work in a quiet and unassuming manner, not caring who got the credit. It is possible that her constituency didn't even realize what a great work she did until she was gone. And she worked according to her ability and means. Dorcas concentrated on what she did best, being motivated by kindness rather than proud ambition.

Dorcas must have been quite outstanding, especially in an era when women seldom achieved status or recognition. Even respect was a rarity. But Luke calls Dorcas a disciple. This phrase could simply imply a follower; but during the early days of the Christian church, the term also designated a teacher or leader, someone respected as part of an elite group. Obviously, Dorcas was much more than a mere follower. In her community, she functioned as a leader.

Luke is the only Gospel writer who speaks of female disciples that followed Jesus. Although he may have been an advocate of women's rights, it is more likely that he wanted to show that discipleship knew no boundaries.

Then tragedy struck. Dorcas became ill and died. Romanticists conjecture that her self-consuming service killed her, but the cause of her death is not mentioned. Her friends, probably mostly the widows from her church, prepared her for burial and laid her in an upper room. They mourned, knowing they had lost their dearest friend.

But before the burial took place, those friends heard that Peter was in nearby Lydda. By now Peter had quite a reputation in the Christian church. He had preached and traveled widely. He had already acquired a certain degree of fame because of the miracles he performed. He was highly respected for his excellent public evangelism and teaching abilities.

Dorcas and Peter may not have been close acquaintances before her death, but perhaps they had met. Whether they had worked together is not known. They do, however, represent how the different gifts of the Spirit, which Paul spoke about in Romans 12:5–8, are valuable in God's church. Peter had those gifts that made him a powerful preacher and leader, while Dorcas exemplified the gifts of service, liberality, and mercy. Both were Spirit-filled workers in the early church, doing much good in their respective spheres of influence.

As Dorcas lay dead in the quietness of an upper room, the widows and her other friends decided to send a message to Peter. Maybe they had a vague hope that Dorcas might be restored to life through Peter's prayers. Maybe they needed the comfort and support of a leading church figure during such a great time of sorrow. Dorcas was a disciple of Jesus and had shown the love of Jesus in her life. Maybe the widows thought they could get help through someone who had actually known Jesus. They recognized that the work of both Peter and Dorcas was inspired by their Master. Whatever the reason, they sent a message for Peter to come, adding, "Do not delay!"

The believers sent two men with this message. For only a distance of eight miles, it would seem unnecessary that they send two people. However, this may have been because of unsafe times and dangerous roads—the two providing mutual protection. More likely, two men were sent so that if anything happened to one, the other could still deliver the message. This indicates just how strongly the believers felt about both Dorcas and Peter.

Peter arrived; the widows met him and immediately took him upstairs. This secluded room was filled with mourners who showed Peter evidence of Dorcas's good work. Confusion must have reigned, what with all the weeping and talking.

No doubt Peter was courteous, but he also needed privacy. Maybe he remembered how Jesus sent everyone out of the room when He raised the daughter of Jairus. So he asked everyone to leave. He needed a quiet, undisturbed atmosphere for the earnest, concentrated prayer he was about to offer. In wanting privacy for this special request of the Lord, Peter showed his dependence on God while he also avoided a display of power. Good deeds need no trumpet blasts in proclaiming what has been done; good deeds speak for themselves.

It's easy to wonder if, besides following his Master's example in praying privately for a miracle, Peter might also have been tempted to say, "Why do you weep? She's only asleep." But Peter had undergone a vast change during his time as a disciple of Jesus. Now he went humbly into the room, shut the door, and prayed earnestly. And a miracle happened.

Peter got up from his knees, turned to the body, and said, "Get up, Dorcas."

Dorcas opened her eyes, and when she saw Peter, she sat up. Obviously, she wasn't startled by his presence and probably greeted him like an old friend. He then invited the mourners in to see her.

Luke writes that "the news raced through the town." No doubt it would! It wasn't every day that someone dead regained life. Why did God work such a miracle? Biblical commentators state that a miracle had tremendous potential in that day. The early church had to struggle against fearful odds. And it could be strengthened by a display of power.

Luke also adds that "many believed in the Lord." Peter stayed in Joppa for a while longer to evangelize the entire neighborhood, while Dorcas probably continued to be "full of good works."

Dorcas and Peter actually worked together for only a short while, but figuratively speaking, they worked hand in hand during their entire ministry. They are a good example of what can be accomplished if the gifts of the Spirit are combined and of what can be accomplished if each person's talents are used for the good of others.

It has been conjectured that Dorcas's example, since she ministered to everyone, regardless of religion, creed, or race, may well have influenced Peter as he related to the racial and religious differences so prevalent in his time. Peter was still in Joppa when he was called by a series of visions to the house of Cornelius, a Gentile. He learned this lesson well, as shown by his later ministry.

Peter and Dorcas also demonstrate the fact that it is not just men or just women who minister, but that all people may work for others through the power of Christ. Through His servants on earth, God speaks to the sick, the unfortunate, and the demon-possessed.

These two leading characters of their time also illustrate another point—the power and influence one Christian can have. It is possible to accomplish much in compassionate action while working alone.

Like Jesus, Dorcas and Peter lived to bless others. We can be equally effective if we are committed to compassionate action.

Chapter 6

Compassion Knows No Boundaries

The morning sun creeps over the horizon. Silhouetted against the light, we see crows and vultures perched on the edges of scruffy and decaying buildings.

As we pick our way over the potholed streets and walk past fetid parks sporting stunted trees, we become aware of sleeping bodies lying in haphazard rows like corpses awaiting burial, covered with tightly drawn dirty sheets, rags, paper, or nothing at all.

Smoke is beginning to lift like a solemn canopy over the sleepers. The smoke comes from wood fires burning on streets or doorsteps that warm a fever-chilled body or a meager handful of food. Bony dogs move away from the sleeping figures stretched out on the sidewalks and cautiously edge toward the warmth of the fires. The odor of the fires mixes with the stench of human waste and motor fumes.

These are some of the sights and sensations we would experience were we to visit Kolkata, India—a squalid city that has changed little since Kipling visited there and called it "the city of dreadful night." Once it boasted pretentious public buildings and extravagant private residences, but decay and neglect have given the city a festering appearance.

Since early times, after it was founded in 1690, Kolkata has attracted rural people who swarm to its streets and become squatters wherever they can find space. Tragically, what most do not find is the stability of a permanent home, a job, an income, and the fulfillment of basic human needs. The starving and homeless stream into the city daily, and conservative estimates put their numbers at five hundred thousand. They keep coming, spilling out of the railway station to settle wherever they can. As a current writer said, "Simultaneously noble and squalid, cultured and desperate, Kolkata is a daily festival of human existence. And it's all played out before your very eyes on teeming streets where not an inch of space is wasted." By its old spelling, Calcutta, India's second-biggest city conjures up images of human suffering to most Westerners. But Bengalis have long been infuriated by one-sided depictions of their vibrant capital.

The sights and smells of Kolkata can hardly leave a person unimpressed by the prevalent human misery. On a street corner lies an elderly man, covered with sores, seemingly comatose until someone passes and he stirs slightly to avoid the footsteps. Huddled by the side of a building are two near-naked children abandoned by their parents. Their eyes are empty, with only shadows of longing and loneliness still evident. A mother stirs a small fire and places on it a pot containing a tiny amount of food. She glances at her clan—a hungry group waiting to share the meager portion.

Into this setting stepped a small, frail young woman many years ago. One might ask, What chance would one person have to make a difference in this hellhole of civilization?

But Mother Teresa did make a difference. Her only qualification for the work she felt called to do was an unquestioning faith in God. Her courageous and indomitable ways drew the attention and admiration of people around the world since she won the Nobel Peace Prize in 1979. But it wasn't always this way. At first she struggled alone with a mission of compassion that showed no signs of eventual success.

Born in 1910 to an Albanian family living in Yugoslavia, she was named Agnes Gonxha Bojaxhiu. By the time she was ten, she knew she wanted to be a nun, and two years later, she also knew where she would spend the rest of her life—in India.

At eighteen, she sailed to this far-off land and for twenty years taught geography and history to daughters of privileged families in Kolkata. The comfortable job, however, only increased her restlessness as she looked out of her convent window and saw the acres of squalor, poverty, and unattended sickness in the slums of Moti Jheel. She grew increasingly disturbed over what she saw. So she did something.

One of her coworkers, Sister Agnes, would later write that their efforts rested on the assumption that "whatever you are doing for the poor, you are doing for Christ."

"It was like that for Mother," Sister Agnes added, "leaving Loreto [the convent] where she was leading a comfortable life for the uncertainty of the streets. She didn't know where she was going, or what she was going to do in the future. Nothing. But she was not frightened. She knew God was calling her and would lead her where He wanted. One thing very outstanding is Mother's faith. She came blindly, trusting in God, not knowing where she was going to live or from where food would come."[1]

For a while, Mother Teresa kept a journal, and before she discarded it, some priests memorized parts of it. One passage describes a long day in which she, while still a sister, spent walking and walking, looking for a place where she could establish a home for the poor and sick so she could care for them. Her arms and legs ached, and her stomach screamed with hunger. She thought of how much a body and soul hurt when looking for shelter, food, and comfort. She was tempted to give up but prayed for courage instead.

She put away her nun's habit and donned the blue-edged

white sari, the dress of India's lowest caste in society. She owned only three of these garments, one for washing, one for mending, and one for wearing.

At first she was entirely alone except for her faith, and the odds seemed insurmountable. Later she was able to say, "Faith is a gift of God. Without it, there would be no life. And our work, to be fruitful and to be beautiful, has to be built on faith. Without faith in God, it would be impossible to face for longer than fifteen minutes the disease and death that we deal with day after day."[2]

She began studying how to provide medical care, because she realized that hospitals would not take in the destitute and wretched who were to become "her people." A story is told that while she was still single-handedly attending to the needs of the poor, a man came to her with a gangrenous thumb. Obviously, she had to do something, so she took a pair of scissors, said a prayer, and cut. The patient fainted and fell one way, and she the other. Eventually, medical ministry became just another part of her extensive work.

In 1950, Mother Teresa set up a new order, the Missionaries of Charity. Although she died in 1997, her work goes on. This religious order currently has 4,501 religious sisters and is active in 133 countries. Many volunteers assist on a long- or short-term basis. Their work extends to countries such as Australia, Spain, England, Italy, and even places in the United States, such as Indianapolis, Miami, the South Bronx, Detroit, Los Angeles, Newark, and Washington, D.C. Workers in these homes take care of alcoholics, prostitutes, shopping-bag ladies, battered wives, the elderly who are sick and needy, and the hungry.

Sometimes Westerners are shocked by the misery and poverty they see in the East, but Mother Teresa found the spiritual poverty of the West equally appalling. And in all places, she said, she found the same thing missing—compassion.

After she received the Nobel Peace Prize, her popularity spread, but she remained the same humble woman as when she first began to fulfill her vision. She traveled to all parts of the world to supervise her work, lecture, consult, and raise money— but when she returned to Kolkata, she plunged in with the rest of her workers. No differences existed as she knelt to wash the maggot-infested sores of a dying person. She rose at four thirty in the morning and was the last in bed at night. When a writer asked her coworkers for legends or anecdotes that would enhance his story, he was told, "There are no legends. The remarkable thing about Mother Teresa is that she was ordinary."[3]

An ordinary, yet extraordinary, life. Many lessons can be learned from this "ordinary" life.

As God's representative, Mother Teresa reflected His mercy. She said, "Let us keep open, ever-forgiving hearts. . . . Then Jesus can use us to radiate His love to others. Then too our love is free of self and truly for the other."[4]

Mother Teresa's display of mercy results in action. Her widespread work that has continued after her death is as complex as that of a multinational corporation and is a testimony of her own unflagging energy spent in meeting the needs of "her people."

Mother Teresa felt responsible to God for her work and actions. When asked, "Do you not grow weary and discouraged when you see the magnitude of this poverty and the small niche that you have made in it?" she replied, "Oh, no. God has not called me to be successful. He has called me to be faithful. And I do what I can each day in faithful accountability to God."[5]

In a success-oriented age, Mother Teresa did not lose her concept of true success. When responding to the congratulatory letters she received after being awarded the Nobel Peace Prize, she said, as she has been widely quoted, "Pray for me that I do not loosen my grip on the hands of Jesus even under the guise of ministering to the poor."

Mother Teresa, while loyal to her church and order, showed that compassionate action should know no boundaries or limitations. She ministered to Protestants, Hindus, and atheists alike. No denominational differences existed when she saw a need.

She realized that her work could not be successful without prayer. An observer once commented that her face was "enriched by prayer." She said, "It would not be possible to work otherwise. There must be a spiritual motive. You can work only for God. You can never work for any man."[6] The amount of time spent in prayer seemed excessive when couched in the hectic days she and her coworkers experienced, but she said, "I am only at His disposal. Without Him I can do nothing."[7]

Mother Teresa believed in the words of Jesus as recorded in Matthew 25:35, 36. "I see Christ in every person I touch, because He has said, 'I was hungry, I was thirsty, I was naked, I was sick, I was suffering, I was homeless, and you took me in.' It's as simple as that. Every time I give a piece of bread, I give it to Him."[8]

She was awed by God's evidence of love to her and sometimes asked the poignant question, "Why these people and not me? That person picked up from the drain, why is he here, why not me? That is the mystery."[9]

Her selflessness is inspiring. When awarded the Nobel Peace Prize, she talked happily of what she would do with it—establish homes for dying destitutes, abandoned children, alcoholics and drug addicts, lepers, and for others of "her people." She was not awed by the honors and awards she has recently received. Even though publicity complicated her life, she said, "Now, everybody knows about the great poverty in the world. People are more aware of the poor and help them more."

Mother Teresa recognized the desperate loneliness and need for love experienced everywhere. She said, "Hunger is not just for a piece of bread. Hunger is for love, deep down in the heart."

She also said that loneliness and the feeling of being unwanted and uncared for are the greatest poverty. This is the reason she established a home for the dying; even if just for a few minutes, these people must know love.

Mother Teresa believed in meeting needs wherever they are. When an American writer interviewed her in Kolkata, she stated, "Tell your American friends they don't have to go around the world to find people who suffer. In America there are many needs. People are lonely. They feel alienated."[10]

Mother Teresa was not perfect, and criticism was no stranger to her. Officials in Kolkata have been known to say she was both a treasure and a nuisance. She was criticized for not delegating enough authority when her work became so extensive. She especially drew fire for her stand on abortion, a practice that never ceases to engender heated discussions. But criticism didn't deter her. One could easily have said, "She should listen and change." But perhaps when her work is placed in perspective, the criticism is not overwhelmingly significant.

Mother Teresa is an example of what one person can accomplish. She believed that if a person does all he or she can, then it is never too little. She said, "We feel ourselves that what we are doing is just a drop in the ocean. But if that drop was not in the ocean, I think the oceans would be less because of that missing drop."[11]

Above all, she held tightly to a relationship with God. "God has given us the opportunity. It is not how much you give, but how much love you put in the giving."

An "ordinary" life, but one that can truly be an example of compassion in action. Mother Teresa was anything but a spectator when it comes to caring!

Endnotes

1. Desmond Doig, *Mother Teresa: Her People and Her Work* (San Francisco: Harper & Row, 1976), 68.

2. Marguerite Michals, "Will Her Work Survive?" *Parade,* February 21, 1982, quoting from Mother Teresa, *A Gift for God* (New York: Harper & Row, 1975), note 4 on page 21, chapter 6.

3. Doig, *Mother Teresa,* 46.

4. Ruth Jutila Chamberlin, "Meeting Mother Teresa," *World Vision,* March 1981.

5. As quoted by the late Oregon Senator Mark Hatfield in "Major Addresses Delivered at the Conference on Faith and Learning," Bethel College, North Newton, Kansas, April 17–19, 1980.

6. Doig, *Mother Teresa,* 155.

7. Ibid., 24.

8. Ibid., 158.

9. Ibid., 162.

10. Chamberlin, "Meeting Mother Teresa," 5.

11. As quoted in *Royal Bank Letter,* vol. 63, no. 2, March–April 1982.

Chapter 7

A Model and a Mandate for Caring

S tevie would sometimes get scared and lonely. After all, he was only ten years old, and a large midwestern city could be spooky at night, especially when the wind howled in from the treeless, wide-open space surrounding the city. Stevie often got hungry as well. Sometimes relatives fed him a meal, and sometimes school friends shared their lunches, but often his stomach rumbled from hunger, and he usually looked pale and lethargic.

Often Stevie spent the night huddled next to the family dogs in the backyard dog house, because he couldn't face the whippings at home anymore. Neighbors reported that they saw him eating fishing worms. He wouldn't go home to eat because he feared the physical abuse that his mother inevitably heaped on him.

When the police finally were alerted to his case, they questioned his mother about his frequent disappearances from home.

"We keep whipping him, but he keeps running to avoid the whippings," she said.

"Where is he now?" asked the policewoman specifically assigned to his case.

"He hasn't been home since yesterday."

"Did you go looking for him?"

"Why should I?" the mother shrugged. "He is ten and old enough to care for himself."

The policewoman, Hulda Roper, then inquired, "Did you ever leave marks on him after a whipping?"

"Sure I have, lots of times," the mother replied.

Stevie was removed from the custody of his mother and taken to a local home for children. Psychological tests showed that he was of normal intelligence, his troubles stemming only from an impoverished, abusive environment. Unfortunately, Stevie's story occurred long ago, in the late 1950s, when people didn't know much about child abuse or how to provide help.

However, working with cases such as these, as well as other cases involving a long list of human ailments, were everyday affairs for Hulda Roper. And for many, she made possible the happy endings they deserved.

Hulda was born to a loving German family in Midwest America. After her father died, she cared for her mother while working diligently for an education. She became a social worker in Lincoln, Nebraska, and took a lively interest in the disadvantaged of her time, yet she was destined to accomplish far more than provide meals for a few destitute families and furnish coal for freezing children. She happened to hear Lincoln's chief of police speak one day, and the possibility of a new and greater challenge occurred to her. After he finished speaking, she went up to him and said, "I'd like to become a member of the police force."

He was surprised. After all, as she later said, "It was such an odd thing to have a woman in the department." But the police chief consented. On June 14, 1944, Hulda became Lincoln's first policewoman. She worked in this role for more than thirty years, and during that time, because of her rare compassionate attitude, compiled a list of accomplishments that cause both admiration and wonder.

She took an active interest in helping alcoholics and in providing programs and humane care for them. "Alcoholics are made during their childhood," she says. "They are sensitive people who have lost control of their lives." She campaigned within her own department for an awareness of the plight of alcoholics. She helped establish a program in Lincoln for the treatment of alcoholics, served on the National Council of Alcoholism board, and assisted with the Alcoholics Anonymous program at the Nebraska State Penal Complex.

Children always had a special place in her life. She was appalled by the way minors were treated after arrest. "You can't believe what it was like," she exclaimed. "Nobody knew about kids. There was no adequate follow-up." After six years of active campaigning on her part, a separate juvenile court was established.

Hulda also showed concern for children who needed a place to go because their own homes were abusive or riddled with other social problems. "We needed a place to put the kids until agencies could decide what to do with them," she explained. She began an active fight for such a home after three children were killed during a fire that leveled their chicken-house home. With community help, the Cedars Home for Children was established and served as a haven for thousands of local children. Although the role of this home has changed over the years, it still functions as a refuge for children in need of safety and shelter.

The sad plight of small children whose parents took them to taverns also bothered Hulda. She campaigned for a curfew law that would at least limit the presence of children in bars. Often she pointed out how parents became too drunk to realize what was going on, and the youngsters were at least neglected, if not harmed. The tavern curfew ordinance was passed.

The elderly and lonely people who lived in rundown apartments on a main street in Lincoln aroused her sympathies. Here lived the people who had fallen through the cracks of society—who had no family, barely enough income from Social Security or welfare to exist from one month to another, who had to live in sparsely furnished rooms and share a bathroom down the hall.

Their plight always concerned Hulda, but at Christmastime it was worse. "They really go off the deep end in loneliness then," she once said. Hulda mobilized community members and groups and for several years brought Christmas to these forgotten people.

One of Lincoln's ethnic groups, Native Americans who had migrated from the reservations in the north, lived in decrepit ghettos on the outskirts of town. Hulda noticed that few had steady jobs, warm homes, and adequate food. Worse yet, their home lives were deteriorating because of the pressures and problems. Hulda and another woman actively worked to assist the Native Americans by making sure the children were in school, trying to find employment for the men, and working with social agencies in meeting physical needs. Not only that, they established programs such as Family Night to keep alive and promote their culture and traditions as well as to maintain family unity.

Hulda had her share of exciting experiences as a policewoman, which have filled a book, but it was her compassionate, active life in addition to law enforcement that impressed many. During her career and after retirement, she received numerous commendations and awards. Her chief once said, "Hulda doesn't become discouraged even when the odds are insurmountable." He then added, "There's no one like her; she's one in a million."

Her work didn't stop after retirement. The Good Neighbor Center in Lincoln needed a new director, and she stepped in. For several years, she supervised distribution of food and clothing, organized classes, and worked with individual cases needing special help.

Even while retired, she still was contacted by people who turned to her or people she had assisted and worked with in the past. Seldom could a conversation carry on uninterrupted, because her phone rang so often.

Hulda retired from an exceptional career in law enforcement, during which she earned the respect and admiration of her peers and community members. But more than that, Hulda had an exceptional record of meeting humanity's needs. During her life and even after her death, she was a model of what one person can accomplish in life if a compassionate vision is part of that life.

A compassionate vision must have been what God had in mind when He spoke through Isaiah about the importance of ministry that not only involves speaking of the gospel but ministering to suffering people. Isaiah 58 is a message for our time as much as it was for Isaiah's.

In this chapter, Isaiah discusses people who outwardly professed to follow God, who wanted to display their virtues and good deeds, and who followed all the rules of religion at that time. But he calls them hypocrites! Their deeds, especially fasting, which they indulged in with self-righteous sorrow and smug superiority, were of no worth because they had forgotten the essence of true religion.

The Jewish religious leaders used fasting as a cloak for all kinds of evil deeds—the Bible speaks of oppression of the widows, orphans, and the poor and of the bribery and injustice that were rampant and affected the less advantaged.

God spoke through Isaiah and said, "Look, what good is fasting when you keep on fighting and quarreling? This kind of fasting will never get you anywhere with me. . . . No, the kind of fast I want is that you stop oppressing those who work for you and treat them fairly and give them what they earn. I want you to share your food with the hungry and bring right into your own homes those who are helpless, poor, and destitute. Clothe those who are cold, and don't hide from relatives who need your help. . . . Feed the hungry! Help those in trouble!" (Isaiah 58:4–10).

The people receiving God's message through Isaiah had forgotten what true religion meant. Even though writings available to them spoke about the essence of true religion, the Jews ignored those messages that didn't concur with their current actions and philosophy of life. The psalmist had written, "He [God] is a father to the fatherless; he gives justice to the widows, for he is holy. He gives families to the lonely, and releases prisoners from jail, singing with joy!" (Psalm 68:5, 6). And a proverb said, "When you help the poor you are lending to the Lord" (Proverbs 19:17). Besides, there was ample description of true religion in the injunctions to the Israelites. But these injunctions didn't take hold in the lives of the Jews. That's the reason for the strong language and firm statements of Isaiah 58.

Is it possible that we are also, at times, somewhat foggy about what true religion is? The apostle James made the basic principles quite clear when he wrote, probably after listening extensively to Jesus and watching Him in action, "The Christian . . . is the one who takes care of orphans and widows, and who remains true to the Lord" (James 1:27).

Undoubtedly, those who suffer from a wide range of problems have been placed close to the Christian church so that our Christianity can be proved and we can develop Christlike characters. True sympathy is the real test that distinguishes true religion from the false. True religion is proved by deeds of love and mercy. We should not become tired of doing good. To avoid compassion fatigue, we need to remember that what we do for others, we do for Christ.

Perhaps against this background, we can outline the principles of the Magna Carta of caring, those fundamental principles described or alluded to in Isaiah 58.

1. God wants an outward expression of religious experience that reflects more than just mere ritual or an adherence

to acceptable religious standards and behaviors.

2. Our expression of religious experience is significantly involved with human relationships, particularly with those who need what we have to offer in terms of humanitarian deeds.

3. These humanitarian deeds are actions that come from love for one another. We must follow Christ's command, when He said, "Love each other as much as I love you" (John 15:12). Paul understood this when he wrote that the whole law of God can be summed up by one command: "Love others as you love yourself" (Galatians 5:14).

4. True religion means an active life of caring for the needs of others. We are to show our inner religious experience by active deeds of mercy, kindness, and compassion.

5. We should not wait for human needs to come to our attention. We should find suffering ones and reach out to them.

6. We must remember just how much compassion for suffering humanity means to God. He has made that one of His commandments for His true followers.

So these are the fundamentals of our Christian behavior—the "Mandate for Caring" as outlined in Isaiah 58. However, being human, we may have a tendency to ask that ubiquitous question, "What's in it for me?"

God has made provision for that. Isaiah 58 includes beautiful promises. Indeed, if our inner religious experience is expressed by compassion and caring, we have many good things we can look forward to!

If you do these things, God will shed his own glorious

light upon you. He will heal you; your godliness will lead you forward, and goodness will be a shield before you, and the glory of the Lord will protect you from behind. Then, when you call, the Lord will answer. "Yes, I am here," he will quickly reply. All you need to do is to stop oppressing the weak, and to stop making false accusations and spreading vicious rumors! . . .

. . . And the Lord will guide you continually, and satisfy you with all good things, and keep you healthy too; and you will be like a well-watered garden, like an ever-flowing spring (Isaiah 58:8–11).

Our active expressions of concern benefit us as well as the recipients of our concern. We are promised health, protection, answers from God, divine guidance, and all good things! While our compassionate actions should not be motivated by the promises in Isaiah 58, we are assured of benefits if our expressions of true religion take the form of tangible action on behalf of humanity.

Two familiar comparisons are used in Isaiah 58 that clinch the point. If we follow the principles outlined, we will be like a well-watered garden and an ever-flowing spring. Both word pictures are familiar to most people. A well-watered garden produces prime quality fruit, is pleasant to look at, and benefits the caretaker. Compassionate human beings, following Jesus' example, are the same. An ever-flowing spring brings relief, furnishes life-giving water to plants and animals, and provides pleasure. The waters are not stagnant but clear and cool because there is action.

True religion isn't just how many prayers we offer or how much of an offering we give or how well we preach the gospel. True religion is expressed in deeds of compassion—it is making concern more than just a spectator sport!

Chapter 8

If We Don't, Why Don't We?

J ust yesterday my local paper ran this headline on the front page: "Paper Salesman Cried Out for Aid, and Cars Kept Passing By."

The news report told of a young man who sold Sunday morning papers on Saturday night. Robert, a twenty-one-year-old student at the local university, was described as clean-cut and industrious.

Sometime around midnight, someone shot him. He staggered, waved his arms at passing cars, and screamed, "Help me! Help me! Somebody please help me!"

A fire department medic and his wife, a nurse, were driving by when they saw him. They said, "We pulled over at the intersection and saw a man bending over. He was screaming." As the couple rushed over to help, Robert stumbled against the building and slid toward the ground. On the front of his shirt was a bloodstain the size of a silver dollar.

Help arrived, but two hours later, Robert died at the local hospital.

The medic told news reporters, "One thing I'll never forget. The cars kept driving by."

Many of us are like the people in the cars that kept going past

Robert. We may remain blissfully unaware of people's needs and therefore go on our own way, while not really meaning to shirk a responsibility. On the other hand, we may have the conviction that we must take caring action, but often we lack courage and a knowledge of just how to proceed. If we're convinced God wants us to make caring more than a spectator sport, why don't we do something?

In the little flower bed that borders our home lives a persistent thistle. It doesn't belong among the trim little bushes and brilliant marigolds. But it persists in making its appearance in spite of efforts to eliminate it. When I walk past this flower bed, I notice the thistle and try to yank it out. It resists, and I can't get enough of a hold on its prickly form to pull it out by the roots.

Yet I seldom want to take the time to get some garden gloves so I can do the job properly. Instead, I break it off, so the neat flower bed will look just right. Then the thistle makes its appearance again. One of these days, when we set time aside to do all the chores around the garden and yard, we will get a tool and take care of this bold intruder, roots and all. Often human behaviors are like that. We need to consider the roots of a problem before we can eliminate it and change course. What are the roots of the problem involving uncompassionate, noncaring, inactive behavior?

1. Many home influences shape us as we grow and become adults. If caring attitudes are not fostered at home, how can caring attitudes be transmitted and disseminated? Sometimes caring is a missing trait in homes because of a disintegrating family nucleus. Sometimes pressures on the parents, both economic and emotional, make caring a difficult trait to nourish.

Thomas Edison was just one individual whose teachers thought he was retarded and stupid. He couldn't seem to learn what they wanted him to learn. His mother, however, had patience. She taught him at home and not only helped develop a keen mind that produced many marvelous inventions of our time, but she instilled in him a keen sense of caring that showed in many ways—such as his concern for bettering the lives of the deaf.

Within the home setting, the trait of caring can be either developed or killed. Most of us struggle, to some degree, with selfishness and self-centeredness. Some believe these are inborn traits and can be eliminated only through effort. That may be, but whatever the reason, the atmosphere of the home can do much to erase noncaring traits and foster attitudes such as Jesus had.

Mary, Jesus' mother, must have done well at nurturing these traits, because accounts of His youth tell us that He developed in wisdom but also in ability to get along with people. Certainly, He showed a great deal of caring for His mother when, as He was dying, He made sure she would be cared for as long as she lived.

2. We are living in an age of detachment, of aloofness, where intellectual activity and technological achievement are sought after energetically. Often, within this milieu, caring is seen as a weakness.

One of my favorite authors, Arthur Gordon, wrote in his thoughtful book *A Touch of Wonder,* "To care, you have to surrender the armor of indifference. You have to be willing to act, to make the first move."[1]

Unquestionably, our twenty-first century marvels are magnificent. And undoubtedly, tangible success is admirable. We live in a better age because people discover cures for physical ailments, invent gadgets that make our lives easier, and improve on the existing contraptions of civilization, giving us more time and pleasure.

But if we forget those who can't take advantage of these technological-age improvements, who don't even have enough of life's blessings to merely subsist, then all these marvels have an empty ring to them. We who claim to be Christians simply can't allow ourselves to forget, as we strive legitimately for success and achievement, that Jesus will eventually say to us, "When you did it to these my brothers, you were doing it to me!" (Matthew 25:40).

3. The old cliché says, "Birds of a feather flock together." Even though this is a worn-out phrase, it's true. We tend to mingle with our class, with those around whom we feel comfortable—with people who "fit."

Of course, our personal "ghettos" are comfortable. And certainly there's nothing wrong with spending time among people who suit us and whom we value. But if we let this behavior develop into exclusivism, then there's a problem.

The story is told of a fishing town on the coast of California that was an ideal location for the area's seagulls. As fishermen cleaned their catch, the seagulls would flock to wharves and gobble up the discarded remains. These seagulls had it easy; the supply of food seemed endless, and they grew fat and lazy. Fishermen came in every evening, cleaned their fish, and the seagulls enjoyed a nightly feast.

Then the business died out. Fishermen moved farther north, and the wharves stood empty. The seagulls stood empty also. They waited and waited for the usual feast. They grew thin. Many died. The problem? They had forgotten how to fish for themselves.

Then some people, humanely concerned about this phenomenon, imported some new birds from another part of the coast. These were placed on the wharf, and they immediately flew over the ocean, filling their bellies with fish. The starving gulls watched. Soon they flew out with the newcomers, and the problem was solved. Integration and interaction with others had taken care of a serious problem. If we insulate ourselves, we may become as spiritually starved as some whom we might help are physically starved.

4. This is an era of noncommunication and insensitivity. Many of our current problems are blamed on television, and while sometimes these accusations are unrealistic, it can't be denied that interpersonal communication skills have eroded because television has robbed us of personal interaction time.

Television also exposes us to human hurts in a way we've never before experienced. We watch everything from a fist splitting a nose to a body being discovered in an alley. Unfortunately, much of this material is in the form of news reports as well as in fictional programs. We are almost required to develop insensitivity, because the human mind has difficulty handling so much trauma in one sitting!

The answers to this problem aren't easy; television is a part of our times. It's only through personal conviction and effort that we can handle this pervasive intrusion that sometimes results in insensitivity. It's easy to turn off the picture and forget what's out there. When we allow ourselves to realize that problems happen to real people—people who hurt—then we can take significant actions.

5. Sometimes our roles as spectators are developed because we lack knowledge of "what's out there." We become insular and parochial, maybe because we simply haven't been exposed to facts and situations that hurt people, and maybe because we are ensconced in our comfortable circles.

Kondiba, a young man in India, was blind because of smallpox. He lived on the fringes of society and eked out a meager living by begging. People shunned him, and he barely existed on the slim income.

One day Kondiba heard a shout of anguish. A child had fallen into the village well! Kondiba didn't know whose child. No one alerted him or informed him of the circumstances.

But Kondiba heard the commotion and groped his way toward the well. Divers tried, in vain, to rescue the victim, with no success. Then, unasked, Kondiba dived into the well. He couldn't see what he was doing; he just groped around. He dived again and again, his lungs almost bursting. Finally, when he felt he couldn't last any longer, he grasped the child. As he surfaced, a cheer went up. The child was saved!

Kondiba retreated to his hut once again, but his life changed. By being alert to the needs around him, he had rescued a human life. As a result, his own life became vastly different. People gave him money, a better home, and work. But best of all, his self-respect grew because all considered him a hero.

To live an insular life is to be uninvolved—to never hear that cry for help.

6. *We live in an uncertain time.* A motorist signaling for help can just as easily be a potential robber or murderer. So we adopt a cautious attitude.

Recently, we were pulling out of a motel parking lot in Los Angeles when a young couple with a child beckoned to us. My husband slowed the car down, and I rolled down the window. The young man leaned his head in and said, "Could you spare some money for us? We've just arrived in town, we can't find a place to stay, the welfare department is closed, and we don't even have money to feed the baby." He motioned to his silent wife and her equally silent bundle.

Our reaction was predictable. Was this a ruse—a setup for some crime? How could we know he was sincere?

Before we could react intelligently, the young man must have read our thoughts. He smiled sweetly and said, "I'm not trying to fool you. I'm a Christian!"

We did react, with a smaller amount of money than later I wished we had shared. So what if the possibility existed that he wasn't telling the truth? The possibility that he *was* in need also existed, and I certainly did have enough that I could share my blessings.

Caution must exist, but let's not become so wary of humanity that we fail to hear a genuine cry for help.

7. *Lately it seems that the daily newspapers and the weekly news magazines are replete with accounts of human misery.* It's overwhelming. Statistics of misery and hurt abound—not just in my

hometown but everywhere! Refugees increase in number each day, hostages and their families hurt unspeakably, children die because of abuse, and so the list goes. What can one person do?

Judy Aitken's attention and prayers turned to Southeast Asia after she saw an emaciated Cambodian child, lifeless in her mother's arms, pictured on the cover of *Time* magazine's November 12, 1979, issue. The look of grief and terror in the eyes of the child's mother resonated with her, a mother of three. She had a strong impression that she should *go* help these suffering people. And shortly after that she saw an opportunity to work in the refugee camps of Thailand.

Those who reached the refugee camps on the border of Thailand made it against all odds. The Cambodians left work camps, the killing fields, caused by the Pol Pot regime. They scavenged food and water along the way to survive, bypassing land mines each step of the dark journey. The Laotians endured hours of swimming the Mekong River, trying to stay underwater as long as possible to avoid the bullets fired from above. The Vietnamese often arrived on boats, narrowly escaping pirate raids and a watery grave.

Judy worked as a nurse in this tumultuous environment. It was like nothing she had ever done before. Then what started out as a short-term mission trip turned into a passion that continues to this day. Judy stopped nursing and began a nonprofit ministry. Between 1986 and 1987, the refugee camps closed down and those who had not immigrated to the United States, Australia, and other countries were forced back to their home countries. Judy had returned to the United States, but her heart remained in Asia. She began refugee projects to help support the work in the war-torn country of Cambodia. In 1995, she founded Adventist Southeast Asia Projects (ASAP Ministries), which continues its work today and has great influence through many countries in Southeast Asia.

Statistics of suffering are indeed enormous, but we must also remember the enormous potential of one person who cares.

8. Even if we do catch a vision of what one person can do, sometimes we lack knowledge of exactly what action we can take. There are no easy answers to this problem of compassionate inaction.

Some years ago, when living in the South of the United States, there lived an interesting man within a few miles of our home. He pushed a bicycle, and perched on this vehicle were large bags of aluminum cans. He was a ubiquitous collector of discarded soda cans. He also was a curiosity—someone to comment on, particularly since on top of the bags was perched a scruffy little dog, his faithful companion!

When I first saw him, I wondered, *Does he do this because he's hungry? Is he lonely? Does he have a home? Just who is he?* And he certainly had a heart, since he walked and pushed the bicycle, but his little furry companion rode.

I discovered that he did live in an impoverished section of a small neighboring town, didn't like women, and made enough of a living to subsist fairly comfortably in his little trailer. I was also warned to avoid him, because, in addition to not liking women, he drank a lot and could be dangerous.

I'm not sure what his needs were and how they could be met. He was one of those puzzling parts of life where a solution isn't exactly obvious.

Situations do arise where it's much harder to see a solution because a simple donation or a friendly Thanksgiving basket simply doesn't seem an appropriate action. In these cases, we must rely on our prayerful commitment to follow Jesus' example, and we will receive wisdom to do the right thing.

9. Sometimes we find it impossible to identify with people's problems and hurts, and therefore we remain indifferent. Here's where the principle of incarnation comes in.

John R. Coleman, at one time the president of a college,

spent many years studying the problems of our country's disadvantaged. Under the disguise of being a blue-collar, impoverished person, he worked in many unusual jobs, just so he could become more acquainted with the needs of these people. He worked at ditch digging and garbage collecting. His most dramatic time, however, was spent as a homeless person in New York City. He wrote a vivid account of this time, when he realized what it really meant to be an outcast, to be unable to find work, to be shunned, and to have to locate warm places to sleep in the streets and live in fear of violence.

John R. Coleman knew what it's like to be a street person. He understood—because he lived like one.

For many reasons, we may not be able to immerse ourselves in the lives of the disadvantaged as Coleman did, but we can make major efforts to achieve some kind of knowledgeable understanding. This is the principle of incarnation—being able to assume a role, to feel what the other person feels, to act as the other person does, and to realize why the other person is the way he or she is.

When Christ came to earth, He was sinless. But He became as one of us sinful beings, and while He remained without sin, He could so identify with us that He died for us. He understood, and He gave Himself.

10. Sometimes we are willing to do all we can on behalf of people who suffer, but we are shy about taking action because we fear being rejected. That is a natural human reaction.

Again, Christ is our Example. He was despised and rejected, the Bible says, yet He never stopped caring.

Rejection hurts, but we should not indulge in self-pity to the point that we stop caring.

11. Perhaps our biggest reason for not caring and putting that caring into action is that we don't have a clear idea of what God expects from us. We cannot remain ignorant of how important compassion and active caring are to God. The Bible is full of commands and examples. Unless we are unaware of the biblical counsel, we have little excuse for our role as spectators in a suffering world.

As discussed earlier, Jesus saw His mission as a twofold one—ministering to souls and also ministering to their suffering. Sometimes in our zealous and well-meaning efforts to evangelize the world, we forget this basic fact.

William Booth, the founder of the Salvation Army, had a unique definition of evangelism—"soup, soap, and salvation." He often reminded his army of workers that they had to feed the hungry before they could share the Bread of Life.

Undoubtedly, these and other reasons explain why we often remain on the sidelines. These reasons may be logical. What isn't quite so logical is our reluctance to get to the roots of our problems. We cannot remain spectators when it comes to genuine caring.

Endnote

1. Arthur Gordon, *A Touch of Wonder* (Old Tappan, N.J.: Fleming H. Revell Co., 1974), 13.

Chapter 9

But the Dog Died Anyway

One dreary fall day, when the rain drizzled just enough to make umbrellas necessary and droopy spirits inevitable, a dog wandered onto our academy campus. Obviously a stray, he sneaked around the corners of buildings, nudged trash cans containing leftover school lunches, and fled from the smug, entrenched faculty dogs.

We ignored him. If we paid him any attention, we said to each other, he'd follow us home, and what then? We couldn't keep another dog! Anyhow, maybe he was just passing through, we reasoned.

The dreary day became a dreary night, and some of us thought fleetingly of the stray dog. Fewer of us had pangs of sympathy and possibly guilt because he must still be hungry, cold, and lonely.

Days passed, but the "mutt" didn't. He stayed on, clinging to the outer fringes of a busy school campus. A few of us wondered just what kind of dog he might be. Certainly odd looking, we all agreed. The American Kennel Club's illustrated book of dogs didn't help. Here was a creature whose rear legs were taller than his front legs, whose hair was mainly black and curly with the exception of a curious fringe of three-inch-long hair jutting out incongruously from the neck, and that didn't sport any distinctive features that might help classify him. We were curious, but it didn't matter if we couldn't find out his mixture of breeds. After all, he was just a stray. Our photography teacher did, however, take his picture. He thought it might make a clever photo for the annual, especially if a cute caption were attached to it.

The dog watched us, probably more than we did him, sitting in a tucked-in, shivering little heap. The drizzly days had turned into bright, sunny fall days, but the mutt still shivered. *Perhaps he's ill,* we mused. But if we took him to the vet, who would pay the bills?

By the end of the week, he had drawn himself closer to the busy doorways and watched us with little dark, sad eyes that peered from beneath a fringe of matted hair. *Ah,* we thought, *he's getting brave. But he still looks ill. Should we do something?* He didn't disappear, and the resident canines who acted as if they owned the campus even tolerated his presence. Once in a while, they condescendingly touched noses, as if to express sympathy or at least friendliness.

But we humans didn't pet him. What if he followed us home? A few of us left scraps from our lunches for him, but we laid them on the steps to the classroom building and quickly went indoors, so he wouldn't get attached to any of us.

By Monday the fall weather turned dreary again. The drizzle fought to steal away our good spirits and won. The mutt had retreated away from the buildings. But he no longer sat and watched; he lay curled up on the rain-drenched grass by the sidewalk leading to the church. Most of us went through the day griping at the weather and the stacks of papers we had to grade— nevermind the increasing chill that promised a damp and inhospitable winter. A few of us still worried about the shivering dog, but our own ill humor consumed our time and interest.

By Monday night the dog lay quite still, and one of us finally picked him up and took him home. But he died anyway. The good Samaritan came to school the next day and told the rest of us, "The dog died. I tried to help him, but he died anyway."

I couldn't get the dog out of my mind. I had the feeling—a rather well-founded feeling—that he had continually asked for our help, and we had refused him.

And I couldn't help but think of a parallel about our behavior—the way we sometimes behave when confronted by a *human* need, whether it be loneliness, hunger, homelessness, illness, or whatever. I think we acted toward that unfortunate mutt very much as we act toward people at times—maybe too many times.

We avoided the stray because we didn't want to be burdened with another dog at home. We knew if we fed him just once or petted him, he'd follow us home, and that would be that. We hoped the problem would go away so we wouldn't have to think about it.

We had become curious about our stray—even looking him up in a book and discussing his features. We didn't get beyond a basic classification—a stray, an unwanted mutt. Were he a human, we'd have probably labeled him as disadvantaged, lower class, a street person.

One of us took his picture, as if to preserve such a unique being for posterity. It could be something to chuckle about a few years later when the school annual would be dragged out. He'd be right there along with the dorm escapades and the swimming parties held during the first week of school.

A few of us threw him scraps of food, but nothing that would give him resistance to illness, make his nondescript coat shiny, and put a sparkle back into his eyes. It was sort of like a donation to charity, meager and quickly forgotten.

We talked about the mutt a lot, and the clowns among us even came up with some pretty good puns. But we didn't take action.

We noticed him, and noticed enough to see he was ill; but none of us felt like shelling out money for the vet bills if we were to give him proper medical attention. Besides, if he got well, then what? What would we do with him?

Finally, one of us tried to help him, but it was too late.

The dog died anyway.

When a few pangs of conscience pricked at us, we wondered, *Was there anything we really could have done for this stray?* He was just one of many, and not a handsome one at that.

A few of us thought about him off and on, but after a few days of sunshine, the drizzle started again, and we forgot about the mutt. After all, the dog had died anyway.

Go and Do Thou Likewise

A t 3:00 A.M. on a drizzly, chilly morning, a young woman stops her van by a garbage dumpster, gets out, and starts sorting through the garbage of a wholesale produce market near one of America's largest cities. She finds what she wants then goes to the dock for more of the same. By 4:00 A.M., she and two friends have filled their van with produce that isn't good enough to make it to a grocery store shelf.

What will she do with such an unsavory load? By 10:00 A.M., the food is cleaned and sorted, and the distribution begins. About 150 needy people line up outside the door of a building that houses a homeless shelter and its services. Along with the produce, these underprivileged people may also receive day-old bread donated by a major bakery, and U.S. government corn-meal.

The activity doesn't stop with the ten o'clock distribution; approximately one thousand people receive food every day.

Groups such as the Community for Creative Non-Violence, Second Harvest, and City Harvest are on the front lines of an effort taking place to salvage discarded food in the United States, yet, unfortunately, these operations manage to reclaim only a fraction of what is discarded every day. Up to 40 percent of our food is wasted every day. Globally, approximately one-third of the food produced for human consumption is wasted. Food banks are trying to minimize this loss while at the same time helping those who desperately need it.

Students are increasingly becoming involved in community-assistance programs everywhere, from prestigious institutions such as Stanford and Harvard to small city- or church-related colleges. It doesn't happen easily, but under committed leadership, students can be motivated easily to participate as volunteers. Besides, as one student says, "We're becoming tired of reading about world hunger, so we can try to put a bowl of soup in front of someone."

An ordinary day could find John Fling of Columbia, South Carolina, delivering pet food to a ninety-one-year-old, nearly blind widow whose thirty-four cats swarm through her small house—or it could find him taking out a loan to keep a landlord from evicting a jobless mother and her five children. Fling was a tireless dynamo who made a vast difference among the needy of his hometown. He cared for the blind, the elderly, the refugees, and the hungry. In fact, when he discovered Miss Flossie, the blind widow, she had no food in the house and was planning to die quietly.

Fling began his ministries in 1947, when he helped operate a string of newsstands and was in charge of approximately one hundred poor paperboys. He never let them go home without a warm coat or a hot meal. Before his death, this ordinary-looking, elderly man collected many awards, and his actions were definitely extraordinary. His widow, who was quietly involved in her own sphere of helpful work, stated, "The Lord gives people different gifts. He gave John the gift of service."

Matthew Cossolotto, a Peace Corp volunteer and former legislative aide in the U.S. House of Representatives, wrote, "Let's face it. America's foreign aid programs have not worked. They have not succeeded in channeling aid to meet the needs of the most needy. They have not been fine-tuned to foster self-help efforts in developing countries." Part of the problem, he says, is that Americans don't have sufficient opportunity to learn about the problems and cultures of the people they are trying to help.

Cossolotto believed in public participation in humanitarian efforts, and along with this he came up with a novel idea. He suggested, "How about adopting a village?" His belief was that a common bond can be beneficially developed between two diverse cultures as represented by a prosperous town and an under-developed village.

Cossolotto had a point. As faceless statistics become actual people, interest and effort increases. Compassionate action can take many forms; caring efforts can be carried out in many ways.

We recognize that only when world peace and universal happiness rule can all problems be solved. Since this is an impossibility until the second coming of Christ occurs, we would do well to consider how we can contribute to solutions and become actively involved in several ways.

First, we should realize that we must have empathy even to understand what it means to be a refugee or a street person or to be similarly underprivileged. This takes interested study; this means discovery of realities that never affect many of us in the United States.

We need to *see* what the problems are and how much they hurt. Unless we make this effort, the faceless statistics will remain just that—faceless statistics. We should have a genuine interest in others. We should seek to understand their needs and give them the help that will benefit them most.

Second, we must be aware of our material and spiritual blessings and be grateful to God. This awareness should lead us to share—to become involved with those who, for whatever reason, have not received these blessings. This means generosity with our time as well as our money. Whether we actually become involved within our own communities, or whether we support programs that assist in faraway lands, we should do so because the Lord has blessed us greatly.

To give personal thought and time and effort will often cost us far more than money. But this is the truest form of charity.

Third, we should try to help people help themselves. In commenting on solutions to the refugee problem, Theodore Hesburgh, past president of Notre Dame University, said, "We are the land of promise, but if everyone who wanted to come here did so, the promise would be very thin and would soon become a nightmare." He and other authorities on refugee problems advocate a committed effort to help by fostering economic and agricultural development.

People can be helped in many ways to overcome dependence on compassionate caring, such as through education and training, programs that involve participation on the part of those helped and develop a sense of caring for each other. Self-help has material as well as psychological benefits, because then we're considering the infinite possibilities of human achievement and development.

Fourth, we can become more effective if we overcome prejudices, biases, and preconceived notions. People needing our help are often "different" and misunderstood. In order for us to really reflect Christ's compassionate caring, we must see needs and problems, not differences.

Value judgments are easy to pronounce. Defensiveness for our own ways of life and accustomed comforts can foster our willingness to sit on the sidelines and let caring become a spectator sport.

For example, although the United States has a long history of welcoming refugees, a wave of objection to this practice is rising. Opening our country to the "huddled masses yearning to breathe free" may not always be the answer, but sometimes it's the only way to spare human lives.

Fifth, we can make caring a habit. This, in fact, is our duty. No doubt many of us would consider it a privilege to visit the Holy Land and walk where Jesus walked. But we do not need to go to Nazareth, Capernaum, or Bethany in order to walk in the steps of Jesus. We can find His footprints beside hospital beds, in poverty-blighted ghettos, in the crowded slums of great cities, or wherever human hearts are in need of hope and sympathy. We can feed the hungry, clothe the naked, and comfort the suffering. We can minister to the discouraged and inspire hope in the hopeless.

And, finally, we should never underestimate what one person can do. Larry Ward, founder of Food for the Hungry International, wrote a book in which he talked about his vision for a program that would help substantially in one area of great need. In *And There Will Be Famines,* he writes, "They die one at a time so we go to help them, one at a time." Awareness of the enormous task of feeding the millions of this world's hungry might have been enough to keep someone from even starting a program, but this did not deter Ward. His organization now reaches into most areas of the world where hunger exists.[1]

On January 13, 1982, Air Florida Flight 90 sat on a runway of Washington's National Airport, stranded in a blizzard. Finally, it received clearance for takeoff, but as it waited its turn, ice formed on the wings.

The passengers joked uneasily and were relieved when the plane lifted off. Among them sat Arland D. Williams Jr., a senior examiner for the Federal Reserve Bank of Atlanta. He had taken a seat in the rear—what he considered the safest part of the plane. Williams considered himself just average, an ordinary person who did his work conscientiously and well but who was not distinguished by anything unusual.

The plane shuddered as it took off and struggled to gain

altitude. It cleared two of the bridges crossing the Potomac, then seemed to stall. Seconds later, it crashed into the third bridge.

Almost immediately, most of the plane disappeared. Only the broken-off tail section remained, and four people clung to this. Another survivor surfaced from the icy water and joined the group of men and women clinging to the jagged metal.

The roar of a helicopter signaled help. A line was dropped to a man about ten feet from the other five survivors, and he reached shore safely. The helicopter returned and aimed the line at a balding man with a gray mustache and sideburns. He caught it but, instead of wrapping it around himself, passed it to another survivor near him. Four times he repeated this action.

By now people on shore and rescuers in the helicopter were intrigued by the drama before them. Who could be so unselfish? Then the tail began sinking slowly. "Hold on!" people cried, but the man began sinking with it.

Twenty minutes after the crash, the chopper once again returned to rescue the last survivor. They searched through the storm, but in vain. The man was gone. "He could have been among the first to be saved," the rescuers said, "but he put everyone else ahead of himself."

Williams helped those within his realm of possibility one by one. He could have put himself ahead of the rest. He could have taken care of his needs first, but he didn't. He helped save four people, one by one.

In considering our responsibility for sharing God's mercy, no specific list of suggestions is possible, because circumstances vary as often as the possibilities for compassionate action. All of us come into contact with people like Eddie, the high school misfit; Malypon, the refugee; José, the migrant worker; Johnson, the street person; and Dee, the abused child. How we choose to help and become involved must be a matter of personal choice and possibility.

One thing, however, is definitely possible. We can add some new phrases to our daily prayers, such as, "Help me, God, to see the world through the eyes of Jesus and to act as He would act. May I never succumb to compassion fatigue. May I ever show my love to You because I'm doing what Christ would do."

Endnote

1. Larry Ward, . . . *And There Will Be Famines* (Glendale, Calif.: Regal Books, 1973), 106.

The Prayer of St. Francis of Assisi

Lord, make me an instrument of Your peace.
Where there is hatred, let me sow love;
Where there is injury, pardon;
Where there is doubt, faith;
Where there is despair, hope;
Where there is darkness, light;
And where there is sadness, joy.
O divine Master, grant that I may not
So much seek to be consoled as to console;
To be understood as to understand;
To be loved as to love;
For it is in giving that we receive;
It is in pardoning that we are pardoned;
And it is in dying
That we are born to eternal life.